ELEMENTS OF THE WILD
A collection of thoughts and poems.

Jade

Copyright © 2019 Jade Carlson

Book design and Editor: Gary Flick

Book cover art: Ashli Temple

Photography for about author: Victoria Bonvicini

ISBN: 9781092630603

For my dear friend, Tracy Stanley. You taught me that my words meant so much. Thank you for your endless encouragement and support.

ELEMENTS OF THE WILD

A part of me died that day. It's like the whole Earth shook and the ground below me broke free to let the wildflowers fill the cracks of everything that was my demise.

I can't tell you how I've come to understand that I don't need to worry about tomorrow, or how I know that everything I want is already mine and it just might take some time for those things to blossom, or how I just started to love for no purpose other than to love. But I can tell you that every day is filled with magic and you don't have to understand things for them to be.

Have you ever wondered what would happen if you freed yourself from all the things you thought you knew and rode the magic of uncertainty and danced with all the endless possibilities?

All I can really hope for, is
that I bring out the magic
that you have locked
inside of you.

I'll always speak my truth, I hope
you can start to do the same.

How many of us
have really seen ourselves
the way that everyone else does?

I touch the Earth,
the Earth touches me,
all I can feel is everything
surrounding me.

If you want to move forward, you
need to accept where you are in
this moment.

Where do you go when no place feels like home? Searching for miles, looking endlessly... when no place sparks that place in your bones, do you hold on to hope or do you choke and settle for a life of mediocrity?

They say you have to learn to live in your own fire; to swim in your own flood; to find your light when the dark is all around you; to just breathe and sometimes let it be; to figure out which wolf to feed and when you need to let them both out to run free.

I sat there for hours wasting time, my own time, the most precious of all. But what is time anyways? It's something that keeps us in a box and gives us the illusion that somehow, if by age whatever, you have your shit together, that you've made it. But you already have made it. You're here. There's no deadline on being who you want to be. You can also change. You don't have to be the same person. You can adjust your ethics to the situation at hand. Is there room for growth? Always.

Are
we
all
just
running
away
from
what
we've
always
been
running
towards?

There was a luminous shadow casting over me, the catacombs of the stardust that filled my bones began to break apart, and then I came to the realization that I was going back to the start.

I have seen another side of me, you broke it free. How was I to see all this before you had left me? It's like you had the key and when I took it back, it unlocked this warm hole inside of me.

Friends vs. Lovers

It's all about connection... and what is a lover, but a friend who helps you find other unexplored parts of yourself? It's an experience. A lesson. Life is full of experiences, it just depends on how you choose to view each one.

If I was going to try to explain myself as a person, I'd say I'm something like this hillside that's covered in paint. A constant work of art. A piece in flowing motion always adding more, and possibly covering something up with another piece of something beautiful. Nothing makes sense, yet it does at the same time, and that's just the way I like it. You'll catch me living life and changing shapes so the pieces will fit into place, but knowing that, at any moment, whatever I love could be erased. And that right there, in and of itself, is wild and beautiful and is what makes me feel free.

My body couldn't take it anymore.

The craving of the closeness of getting right there to the edge, to just be slung all the way back to the start.

To almost having it, but not quite... maybe that's what makes us appreciate things more or appreciate things in the moment more.

Be here now. Be here now.

Is our history what we are? Because sometimes I can't recall whether moments in my own mind are real or false. If everything is an illusion, then how come my chest caves in at times? Emotions rip thru me and drip down my spine, seeping into every crack and crevice in my skin from ages of wear and chasing the sun, using my body like a machine... which, I mean, I guess it technically is.

Who I am depends on who you ask,
and if that's not beautiful, I don't
know what is.

I was once told girls my age never mean what they say, but who are you to tell me to not let my emotions get in the way? After all, that's the only way you feel anything anyways.

Have you ever pulled the sheets back on your own life? Uncovering all that has been hidden and exposing things for what they really are? To look into the eyes of everything you know and question if it's all actually bullshit? Well let me tell you: sometimes it is. Sometimes it's all bullshit, and sometimes that bullshit ends up being the bullshit you need to make a change in your life.

I crave connection; the constant electricity between two humans; the way we have the ability to adapt and evolve with each other; how we can look past all their insecurities and see this beaming light; how some of us are so quick to just give up everything for another human, yet somehow can't figure our own shit out.

Girl of the Wild

They told me to behave, but that's something I could never do.

I couldn't keep the words from spilling, just like you couldn't stop believing you loved the life you were leading. Things can be kind of deceiving and happen for no rhyme or reason, just like people change with the seasons.

It wasn't until I was at the
darkest
part of myself that I found my
light.

One day love was just there, like it had been standing at my front door screaming, "Let me in." And that's because it was right there all along… inside of me just waiting to burst open at the seams.

It's all about movement, change, and not staying stagnant. Sometimes you gotta go against the current to really learn the lesson. And at times you'll have to peel all these oniony layers of yourself back to see the real you at its core and realize the real you is full of fucking magic and whomever can't see that will never be enough for you.

Who am I?
What am I?
Am I more than all these layers of skin?
More than all these layers of conditioning?
More than all these things I've
convinced myself that I am?
There's more than all of it. I know it.

I put it all on the line
all the while you were fine.

I'm always traveling towards an
uncertain future.

I'll remember the good ol'
days and getting myself into
messes and all the stresses
that I didn't know were
lessons and blessings.

Everyone runs away.

I won't be a scratch post for your fears
and insecurities.

I thought it was something more than your thoughts being consumed by the flame of the chatter in your brain. You made feel me insane but you were the one still speaking my name.

It's a never-ending journey of unbecoming myself and finding myself, a constant ebb and flow.

When the dust settled
you were a haiku to me
not anything more

Is it wasted time? And what is trust when everything is shifting anyways? Nothing stays the same. It's an ever-changing game, like chasing fireflies at sunset as a kid.

The sun was shining so bright that I thought for a moment *what would it be like to be completely engulfed and taken in by the flames of the sun?*
Then I realized: *I am that fire. I am that burning sensation. I am everything. Everything is a part of me.*

Spain/Portugal

I don't think I'll ever have the right words to say what this trip meant to me. Thank you for making me lose myself and find myself again; for reminding me that love is and has always been the answer for me. To just love… to love the good to love the bad and to love yourself and others without holding back anything; for reminding me that people can only meet you as far as they have met themselves, but that doesn't mean they have any less love in them than you do. We're all on different paths, but if we continue to do things out of love instead of fear and hate, the world would be a better place, because what you fear and what you hate are just projections of yourself. So put a smile on your face, and if you're looking for your next love, look in the mirror.

There's an urge in me to feel
everything until it becomes numb,
and in the beginning I can never
figure out how to word it, 'cause
it's too soon to say "perfect," but
that's how it feels... that ecstasy
takes over and I never know if I
should ruin it or let it ruin me.

I had been before, but I knew I had
to come back…. the sunsets man…
the sunsets.

If you told me that the swelling tides in my chest were false, that they were just these infinite streams to connect us to each other like tree lines off in the horizon, spaced apart close up, but from afar looking like one. Things are like that, though... the way things appear to be something else. I think I'll keep being transparent.

Just like other things,
I think I always knew your
love was something that I
could never win.

Infinite cosmos spinning
around us until we
disappear.

Just when I think I've
figured myself out, I'm out
the door running to
reinvent myself

I have always lived free, but at times find myself caged in these "cages" that I essentially made for myself. I do it to let myself know what comfortability is, to remind myself what it's like to fixate on something or someone, to let myself feel love, feel happiness, feel pain, to feel the human experience, to draw maps of my loneliness and trace the goosebumps on lovers' backs, to make myself stay in one spot longer than a few months. We all cage ourselves in for reasons we sometimes don't understand, but we always hold the key to letting ourselves be free.

Is it that important?

One day you can fall asleep and
never wake up again. Any day,
any moment could be your last,
and how that doesn't make people
want to wake the fuck up and
start living their lives scares the
shit out of me.

What is so important that it's
keeping you from living your life?

Living Wild

I've come to realize my absolute favorite thing is good company in an open space, there's just something about being out there and really getting to connect to the people you're with, without all of the distractions. You can feel all the layers of society peel off. Screaming your favorite songs at the top of your lungs, running naked thru the desert during the full moon, late night hot spring adventures, taking your car on roads that you 100% should not be driving on, getting lost hiking for seven miles, skinny dipping in the river, driving 16 hours so you can watch the solar eclipse, waking up in Yosemite in a car filled with fart smells from your road trip partner, locking your keys in the car when you're basically in the middle of nowhere. Those are the things that make me feel the most alive.

It was creeping up my spine,
inch by inch, until it made a
home in my bones.

My feet can never stay still.
I was never one who could just look outside
from the windowsill. I needed to feel what I
was seeing, to know the feeling so I could
believe what my eyes were seeing.

Creating My Own Wonderland

I was riding the wave of potentially falling down any rabbit hole that presented itself to me. It's like everything was a blur, I was in some trance.

I got a bad habit of pulling you in
closer when I'm trying to run
away.

When you're friends with
someone for the right reasons,
there are not many issues.

Sometimes I forget to really live in the moment and sometimes I get caught up living too much in the moment. If all I have is now, then why face anymore bullshit? Why spend any more time waiting around for someone else to figure out their bullshit and why do I keep getting myself stuck in these same bullshit patterns? It's all bullshit anyways.

You were never mine, can't say I didn't try,
finally realized the real lie was that I was blind.
Thought things were different this time
but I was my own demise.

Things are always happening times are always changing. Some of us spend a lifetime trying to get it right but are blinded by our feelings inside only later to see things in hindsight.

Paint me with the colors of your life.

Staring at the night sky
counting the stars
laying in your back yard on the
trampoline.
We were invincible back then.
Thought we were kings and queens.

Do I live my life how I
want or conform to
everyone else's reality?

The most painful and beautiful art is letting go.

Three

Three months of nothing.
Three months of shame.
I didn't even realize how frequently I was speaking your name.
My stomach in knots, my heart consumed by my thoughts.
Do you ever step back and wonder how you became so distraught?
I was told this wouldn't hurt a lot, I guess not.

My life has become my muse.

How dare you say
I was in the way
when you were the one
who made my light fade away

It's All Nothing; It's All Everything

How often do you lose your balance? Do you love the feeling of having nothing left to lose? If everything is fleeting, then nothing is everything and everything is nothing. The thoughts that consume my mind are the ones that probably eat yours alive. Can you hold your composure and move a little closer to the universe that's inside my mind waiting to be explored?

I've spent a lot of time in love, to only have it ripped out like the tide.

Life happens in motions,
like the ocean
coming and going in waves.
Whenever you get stuck in a daze,
remember: even the ocean
gets stuck in its own undertow
only to resurface again.

I want someone with
soul
passion
emotion
and so much love
in their heart that
they might explode
if they don't get it out

2017

I sometimes get an extreme longing for going
to new places, meeting new faces and
somehow blending myself into these lines that
weren't made for me. I've spent a lot of time
reflecting on 2017 and how I spent most of it
with my most prized possessions tucked away
in my trunk while I hopped around the whole
state of California blindly searching for
anything that would make me feel alive and
rebellious. LA was home but I couldn't stay
there long enough to ever build a solid
foundation. Always seeking something more
because I knew there was more than what that
city had to offer me. I was never going to find
myself there. I was convinced the open road
had the answers and I would find them.

Keep living the best you know how to.

That's the funny thing about life though, the contrast, how you can't have one without the other. Light and dark.

The good, the bad. The flipping your perspective. Knowing to trust that it's a work in progress, it's art, it's a constellation of you and it takes working at it every day.

We were strangers whose silhouettes exploded
with stardust, taking us into another world
even if just for some time.

If there is any advice that I could give...

It's that you'll always be too
much for someone who is
not enough for YOU.

Jet lag in my eyes
stuck in a haze
lost in a daze
riding out the wave
getting caught up in the
night time
making things out of nothing
thought it was the way
to become something
nothing to lose and ready
to take off at the push of a button
starting over with the season
and not giving two shits
what's the reason
there were roses on my dress
and I honestly don't know
who I was trying to impress
I told them I was catching flights not feelings
but what I really need was some healing
from the lines I was believing

I want to
say that
I'm here
to stay
but I can
feel
myself

fading

away.

Magic happens

I can't be scared because I know the universe
has a plan and my being is a part of something
so much more than any of us could ever wrap
our brains around. Whatever comes my way is
a path to a better me, even if the lesson doesn't
present itself for years to come. Just trust in the
universe and watch the magic happen.

It's the things that we are afraid of that make us who we are... or at least some of us. Some of us chase the things we fear, while others run and seek safety. Some of us name our fears, and some leave them nameless.

Always leaving when I'm close to comfort.

Moments overlap and time has become
an illusion.

I can hardly remember the way you
taste
Never acting my age, but
shit, what's age anyways?
Not much to lose 'cause
I'm hardly hanging on
Man oh man, I can do what I want
Recently it's been chasing the rising sun

Views

It baffles me how people can be so caught up in this image they have created for themselves. Something completely made up. To be so set in your ways that you can't switch your perspective to see how another person may view things or how you even view your own.

Every time I start to get comfortable, the universe is there to remind me that there are endless possibilities and that I can never get caught up living in one type of way.

I'm back to tending the garden of my own thoughts.

It hasn't been hard
but it hasn't been easy
the feelings come
and go in waves

How can I feel so at peace in a place that is so foreign to me? If I'm meant to be here... this is it. No more running up and down the coasts hoping to find something. I lose a piece of me every time I board a flight, take a long road trip, start something new, etc. Sometimes I gain but then I let go. What is letting go? What is holding on? Why do either? Just let it be.

So many wants that I don't even know
what I need.

The light hit my eyelids
in a way that made me feel
like the sun swallowed me
up whole and I had became
the light itself.

Sometimes I think I know what I want
and other times
                        I'm pulled
                                    towards
something else

I sat there watching the water drip down the cascade wondering how things could have ended up this way. Then I saw the moon and howled my lungs out.

Always chasing, always wanting.

There will come a day when you'll find my body burning on the mountain side with wildflowers in my hair.

Day by day do you ever wonder
what you're holding on to?

 Not saying the things worth
saying because you're afraid?

Afraid of what, though?
Everything is fleeting.

Nothing lasts forever. Relish in the
moment.

Shifting

I have felt the shift happening for a while now.
I couldn't really put my finger on what it was,
but I now know I'm shedding older versions of
me and keeping the parts that make my heart
sing.

I want to breathe your fire again.

What a beautiful thing it is that we're all just spinning on this thing called Earth. Not really in control of anything. Not really knowing what the hell we're doing here at all. We're all lost in these ideas and beliefs that we've evolved ourselves into believing to be true. Break Free.

I peeled the freckles off my skin
and kissed your shoulder blades
as the tide rushed in.

Time waits for no one. Show up as the best
possible version of yourself every day.
For yourself.

There was so much I needed to learn, but at that age I thought I knew it all. Back to being the villain in my own story who somehow still ends up soaking in her own glory.

I carry everyone from my past
with me

Time flies by faster than a
bullet spitting out of a gun.

All these years I thought
you were the one.

Sometimes I don't always
make sense, but to some
I always make none.

It was all mine for the taking. Then I thought how could I have been so mistaken to let a vacation mask the sensations that my heart and brain were making.

I think people forget that they can
rewrite their plot.

We could have been so
much more than friends.

One string but living on
opposite ends.

I never know which way to go.

Constantly being pulled in between
the two worlds and lives that I want
to lead.

Where is the balance?

I don't know if I'll ever have it.

Only now do I
know this feeling as
changing.
Growing into
something better.

I don't need to find
love in other people
when I have it in
my own bones.

I don't think we can exist without
the contrast. We all have good
and bad, dark and light sides.
When we enter our darkest
times/path, it's also the path that
brings us to our most enlightened
moments as humans.

That summer sun must have had me confused.

I didn't realize I was only being used to amuse the curious side of you.

I've done it again.
I tried to blur myself into a line that
wasn't made for me.

The mind is as wild as the West once
was.

Sometimes I cry when I sit
down with my own and try
to convey my words to a
rhyme.

I question everything way too much and I can't decide where to draw the line.

Is it a good thing or is it a terrible thing that my brain is constantly wondering in all directions?

It's here, it's there, it's everywhere.

I tried to tell you
we were dreaming
so I drew a map and an
x that marks the spot
but you had already
decided to make things
come to a halt.

I held your hand as
you watched me fall.
Tell me, does my ghost
still linger inside your
four bedroom walls?

I don't think you could stop it any more than I could.

Sometimes, despite how hard you try to stop it, magnetic things will be pulled back together.

I was born to run free
to change who I want to be as I please
to adjust my ethics to the situation at hand
No one controls me
I was not meant for one place
I was born restless
and the world outside
my comfort zone is
constantly calling me saying
"come run wild and let your spirit play"

These things I feel
cannot be put into
words

 I can only hope to
be the sweet honey

dripping from your
fingertips or the
moon

that lights up your
darkest nights

Day by day do you ever wonder what you're holding on to? Not saying the things worth saying because you're afraid? Afraid of what though? Everything is fleeting. Nothing lasts forever. Relish in the moment.

Your perception will change literally everything.

I'm starting to think that the best parts of life are a collection of all of those moments where you pushed yourself past your limits. All those times you thought "I shouldn't do this" but then you said "fuck it" and decided to live.

It's divine knowing time is only an
illusion.

Once the foundation of who I was conditioned to believe I was started crumbling, I saw the truth behind all those layers. I was everything I already needed to be.

The smooth roads will never be the ones that bring you to your truth.

I've stretched my skin along
this coast, forming lines to
tell stories of horrors and
glories.

If you never challenge what you see,
your life will continue to only be
mediocre and boring.

I'll flow with the water into an eternal ever after, floating there feeling the being. The cells divide, gather, and then multiply.

I hope you treat every day like a blank
page.

We were trying to make homes in each other's bones.

You'll always be a part of who I was in the past.

The boys of the highway always made me scream and shout, "I don't give a fuck" while hanging out the top.

I believed in everything you're not.

Comfortability has become a stranger.

A flip of perception means a change in direction.

Always choose experience over being
content.

I'll always end up just where I'm
headed.

My bound is as limitless as the stars.
I will no longer starve myself of the
possibilities that await on any given day.

What a feeling to know the world is at
your fingertips.

The moon made my worries melt
away like honey dripping down
my spine. She was telling me
everything is going to be fine.

I'll continue to crack and let the light fill
every void.

Stop letting people become your ceilings.

What if the only road you've ever known is always changing? How are you ever supposed to know which way will lead you home?

You have to realize that to truly find
yourself you're going to have to
come undone thru and thru.

If you really want to be free....
You need to run far from all that you've
ever known.

I think things are a lot simpler than I make them out to be in my head.

Made in USA - Kendallville, IN
1220004_9781092630603
12.30.2020 1104